THE CONCISE HISTORIES OF DEVON

CROMWELLIAN
AND RESTORATION
DEVON

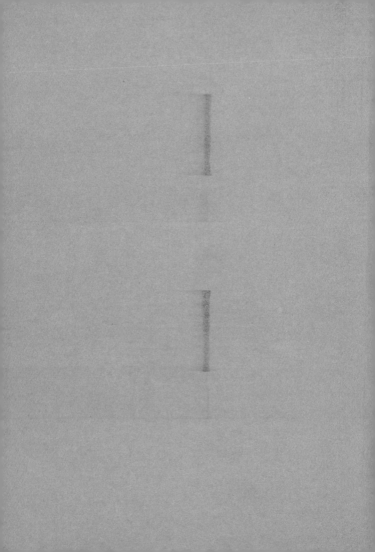

THE CONCISE HISTORIES OF DEVON

CROMWELLIAN
AND RESTORATION
DEVON

THE
MINT
PRESS

IVAN ROOTS

First published in Great Britain by The Mint Press, 2003

ISBN 1-903356-30-x

Cataloguing in Publication Data
CIP record for this title is available from the British Library

The Mint Press
18 The Mint
Exeter, Devon
England EX4 3BL

Cover and text design by Delphine Jones

Main cover illustration: General Monck (courtesy of Exeter City Council)

Coin: ½ crown, Charles II, 1670 (courtesy of Exeter Museums Service)

Printed and bound in Great Britain
by Short Run Press Ltd, Exeter.

CONTENTS

DEVON AND THE INTERREGNUM

The New Model Army's victories across Devon in 1646 destroyed Charles I's military hopes. A captive, successively of the Scots, Parliament and the army, he turned to policy by other means, playing enemies (and even his friends) off against one another in a fruitless search for a settlement. The result in 1648 was a second civil war, widely fought. But Devon, though considered a likely base for a royalist comeback, was not directly involved. The county itself was preoccupied with its own search for a settlement, a return to normality against the background of the depredations of the war and of current ills, not least the weather. The later 1640s saw poor harvests, food shortages and visitations of the plague, striking Barnstaple in 1646 and Totnes in 1647. All this was accompanied by a continuing oppressive military presence, garrisons maintained by high taxes in the towns, with free quartering and pressing in the countryside, too. That officers could be sensitive to local susceptibilities, ready to co-operate with JPs and town chambers, did not drive away discontents. Townsfolk who had fled royalist occupation and parliamentary sieges were slow to return. In most places pre-war populations were not reached again until the end of the century. But traditional local authorities carried on in as much of the old way as was possible, even allowing themselves occasional bursts of factional politics. Optimistically Devon towns and villages prepared accounts of sums expended in the late wars, sending them up to London for reimbursement. They would be disappointed.

In December 1648 the Commons was purged by Col. Edward Pride of MPs urging continuing negotiations with the king. Devon's representatives, for the most part Presbyterian (to the right in politics and religion), were conspicuous among those excluded. On 30 January

1649 Charles was executed. Soon, the House of Lords was abolished and a (republican) Commonwealth established under a sovereign Rump of a parliament. Only one Devonian, Gregory Clement of Plymouth, MP for Fowey, was a regicide. He would pay the price for that in 1660.

These astonishing events excited little outward display of either joy or dismay in a subdued Devon. Out of respect for the martyred monarch Tiverton chamber briefly replaced scarlet robes for black. The mayor of Exeter, who refused to read out the proclamation of the new regime, was suspended. Barnstaple spent £22 on new civil regalia, including a mace with republican symbols, a seeming revolutionary gesture, but, after all, a mace is still a mace. An engagement of loyalty to government 'without king and peers' required of all males of 18 and above appears to have been generally taken across the country. The legal beagle John Maynard, a 'secluded' MP, subscribed to ensure the continuance of his high legal fees on the Western Circuit, setting a pattern for his unsinkable future.

While Oliver Cromwell, up and coming, completed the conquest of Ireland – where Devonians from Drake and Raleigh on had an interest, supporting the English Protestant ascendancy and, as 'adventurers', land-hungry – and of Scotland, Devon was still quiet. There was no support for the Prince of Wales's invasion from Scotland in 1651, nor for the exiled Sir Ralph Hopton, who from the Channel Islands 'vented his fury' on Commonwealth shipping. Admiral Robert Blake soon stopped that.

In April 1653 Cromwell threw out the Rump, enforcing a transition from the Commonwealth to a Nominated Assembly, including half-a-dozen Devonians. It turned itself into a parliament, ('Barebones'), with the prominent scholar and politician, Francis Rous of Tavistock, as Speaker. Disappointing and disappointed, the Assembly soon resigned (December 1653), to be replaced immediately by a Protectorate under (who else?) Cromwell, with a written constitution, 'a single person', a council of state and a parliament elected on a new franchise with a revised list of constituencies, reducing the number of 'pocket'

boroughs blatantly open to the influence
of the gentry. One speaks here of John
Maynard, hitherto nursing 'his' borough
of Bere Alston. But substantial gentlemen
like Sir John Copplestone, Robert Rolle,
William Morrice (a former Rumper
sheriff) and Thomas Bampfylde of
Poltimore, Recorder of Exeter, 'the
spiritual heir of Ignatius Jourdain',
Exeter's gift to puritanism, did get
themselves into the first parliament (1654-
5). Proving uncomfortable to the
Protector, it was after five lunar
months abruptly dismissed, having done
nothing constructive.

Continuing a policy initiated by the
Commonwealth, Cromwell made a genuine
attempt at conciliation by naming to his
first Commission of the Peace for Devon a

diversity – some 'new' men, certainly, even outsiders, but also 'old' gentry, including a few too young to have fought in the war. There were lawyers, merchants, too, and, of course, military men. Not all nominees responded; that was not to be expected, but some could not resist, even in these changed circumstances, to take the opportunity glimpsed to play their traditional role in the community. Supposing that the new régime might become permanent – and why not? – they saw little reason to deprive themselves of the challenges and advantages, communal and private, offered. The names Drake, Pollexfen and Rosewell crop up.

In military command of the south west was Cromwell's brother-in-law, John Disbrowe, based in Exeter. He had taken a moderate line, working towards the formation of a county militia to relieve the burden of military expenditure on both central and local government. But Disbrowe was no pushover. In 1653 he threw out some Tiverton councillors as 'scandalous in their lives' as well as apparent dangers to security. But he looked for co-operation from J.P.s and local officials, not only for the maintenance of security, but for the implementation of routine tasks such as the poor law, bridge and highway maintenance and suppression of public nuisances.

Disbrowe's control was severely tested in March 1655 when John Penruddock led a small band of royalists into Devon from Wiltshire, hoping by their example to raise the south west. But recruits were not forthcoming. Diverted to South Molton, they were swiftly rounded up by a combined regular and (significantly) militia force. At Exeter the leaders were executed in exemplary fashion. Lesser men were transported as forcibly indentured servants to the English colonies in the Caribbean – an innovation in crime control that would become one of the few permanent consequences of the Interregnum. (Some Devonians would go there and to North America as free men and women, cheerfully seeking their fortune).

Penruddock's rising had a striking effect. Fearing universal royalist attempts, in August 1655 the Council of State divided England and Wales into a dozen areas – 'cantons' – each under a major

general, assisted by local commissioners,
charged with military security and social
control. The major generals' detailed
instructions were based on what Disbrowe
– now given the six south western counties
– had already been doing in Devon. What
was new was 'the decimation tax' upon
known and suspected royalists, whose
movements were also closely monitored
and registered. Each 'swordsman' – they
were a heterogeneous lot – gave his own
idiosyncratic priorities to the detail of his
instructions. Some were heavy-handed,
particularly in implementing a 'godly'
moral programme. Disbrowe was more
lenient, still seeking and getting, a decent
support from his commissioners, a
mélange of 'old' and 'new' men, and from
the routine administrative and judicial

authorities. Disbrowe's register of royalists
giving bonds for their travel was strikingly
effective. A survival of a sense of
community is glimpsed in John
Copplestone's gesture to the royalist Sir
Edward Seymour, 'as a person of worth
and honour', promising to be 'as civil as
[he] possibly can' in the decimation.

But the experiment across the country
had proved highly unpopular. Disbrowe's
promotion of 'a short bill' in the second
protectorate parliament (September 1656-
February 1658) for the continuance of the
decimation was assailed. It – and the whole
'system' – was quietly dropped, not least
because the Protector himself had come to
see in it a bar to 'healing and settling' which
he had set as his prime task. Cromwell's
régime was moderately tolerant in religion,

too tolerant for some even in his own government. The 1640s Presbyterian system had collapsed. It was replaced by a loose national church on Congregational lines. Two commissions, the one of Triers, the other of Ejectors, men lay and clerical of a wide range of persuasions, were set up to consider the qualities of parochial ministers. Generalisations about incumbents in this period are difficult. Not every 'orthodox' Anglican had been turned out in the late 1640s; some would survive the Protectorate. The Act of Uniformity of 1662 would bring back others, while purging intruders. There were, of course, thoroughly radical sectarians for whom no extraneously disciplined church, least of all one maintained by tithes as was the Protectorate's, was acceptable. Appearing

among them in the early 1650s was a novel
amorphous group, driven by an individual
inner light, defiant of constituted
authorities and regarded by sober men as
destructive of the social order. Springing up
everywhere and particularly in Devon, they
were called Quakers, not yet the plain,
quiet, hardworking Society of Friends of
later years. In October 1655 a former
parliamentarian soldier turned Quaker,
James Nayler, was released from prison in
Exeter. From there he set off on a journey
to Bristol culminating in a symbolic re-
enactment of the entry of Christ into
Jerusalem, with women casting down palms
before him. This 'horrid blasphemy' came
to the attention of the Commons. There
Nayler was charged, tried, condemned and
punished – by branding. These actions by

the Commons raised far-reaching constitutional issues in debates, long and deep, which led on to another written constitution. A seemingly trivial incident emanating from Devon had somehow provoked a national crisis. The new dispensation, producing a second chamber – 'the other House' – to act as a check upon the judicial claims of the Commons put forward in 'the case of James Nayler', proved a failure. History – even local history – is, indeed, a record of the unexpected.

Down in Devon the Quakers pressed on in spite of persecution from magistrates acting with popular support. The quarter sessions in 1658 ordered a ban on their books. Barnstaple's records report sending down two Quakers to Exeter gaol for incarceration. Quakers grew strong in Topsham and in 1657 were bold enough to hold a general county meeting in Exeter.

When Cromwell died on 3 September 1658 an expected general royalist rising failed to materialise. Richard Cromwell was proclaimed Protector across Devon. Barnstaple fired a salute on guns hired from Appledore. In Exeter the chamber processed colourfully in Richard's honour. In his parliament (January 1659), called on the old franchise, Devon again had its plethora of MPs, a more than somewhat eclectic lot, including some certainly crypto-royalists. As Speaker, Thomas Bampfylde had to cope with the handsome delaying tactics of republicans in interminable debates over the legitimacy of the Protector's title. Exasperated, the

Grandees of the army forced Richard to
dissolve the parliament. Soon, very
sensibly, he resigned, leaving the generals
to squabble over what was now to be done.
As a stop-gap, they recalled the Rump.
Devon again lost most of its
representation. The Rump was thrown out
and recalled again. Throughout 1659 the
country seemed to be sliding inexorably
into anarchy, raising fears in shires like
Devon of a recrudescence of civil war. In
Exeter, which had been refortified in 1658,
there were disorders in the streets, and in
rural areas hints of 'a flame in the west' lit
by impatient royalists. Into this fraught
situation an enigmatic Devonian, General
George Monck of Great Potheridge near
Torrington, a former royalist turned
Cromwellian, now commander-in-chief,

effectively governor, of Scotland decided
to intervene, crossing into England on 1
January 1660, with an army – 'George's
Boys' – well-paid and therefore well-
disciplined, unlike the rank and file in
England now contemptuous of their
quarrelsome officers. On a slow march
down to London – that vital organ –
Monck met deputations petitioning for 'a
free parliament' – code for a return to
monarchy. Some came from Devon
inhabitants 'groaning under high
oppressions and a general defect of trade'.
Erstwhile parliamentarians were now
metamorphosing into neo-royalists. Even
before the end of 1659 it was rumoured
that the military governor of Exeter was
already in touch with the exiled king.

Monck, not a typical Devonian, so

secretive that 'even his shirt was not privy
to his thoughts', said nothing. His wife, a
convinced royalist, said rather more. But
'Black Monck' without committing
himself, was in touch with a mixed group
of Devon royalists – Sir John Grenville,
William Morrice, his own brother
Nicholas, themselves in close contact with
those in exile - urging them to be patient
and circumspect. Arrived in London
(February) he quickly 'persuaded' the
Rump to readmit Pride's 'secluded
members', increasing the size and
influence of the Devonian group there.
(A Devon petition had blamed 'all our
confusions' on the Purge). Once back, no
longer the Rump, the Long Parliament at
last legally dissolved itself, arranging for a
speedy election of a Convention

parliament on the old franchise, with House of Lords included. On 25 April it voted that 'the Government is and ought to be by King, Lords and Commons'. Meanwhile garrisons in Devon, including Plymouth, were in the hands of Monck supporters. Everywhere opposition was melting.

Monck was now directly in touch with the king, to whom – he would, wouldn't he? – he claimed he had been 'always faithful but never in a condition to do him service till the present time'. Tactfully, Charles 'believed' him and recognising that Monck and his Devonians had his fate in their hands, accepted advice to issue a conciliatory declaration from Breda, offering something to almost every 'party' (4 April). This was presented to the

Convention by Grenville. Charles was back in London by the end of May. The Restoration was already being celebrated in Devon with parades, gun salutes, banquets and, as usual, bonfires. Charles was proclaimed at three places in Exeter in a solemn procession, the chamber in scarlet – reminiscent of the proclamation of Richard – with bells ringing, banners, conduits flowing with wine. At Tiverton on 29 May an elaborate anti-Cromwell ritual was instituted, which would be annually performed for long years to come.

Whether Monck's coup was some consummate instance of 'the art of restoring' or simply a pragmatic response to events is a question. But the significance in all this of Devonians is incontestable.

'Victor sine sanguine', Monck received his rewards – the dukedom of Albemarle, (the Moncks claimed Norman and Plantagenet descent), the earldom of Torrington, mastership of the King's horse, and whatever. He could have demanded more – and got it. As earl of Bath Grenville became Governor of Plymouth and Lord Warden of the Stannaries, an increasingly honorific office. Knighted, Morrice got a secretaryship of state. Nicholas Monck settled comfortably in as Provost of Eton. All this and what followed by way of settlement were the history of England, but they were also the history of Devon. Not for the first time nor the last the two were intimately intertwined.

DEVON
ECONOMY
AND
SOCIETY

Among the largest of English counties, Devon is topographically remarkably diverse. Placed between two seas, north and south, with land boundaries to east and west, it looks both inward and outward. Two great 'wildernesses', Dartmoor and Exmoor, wooded hills, broad river valleys and many bays and beaches have made for a region more than a shire. So it was in the seventeenth century. History had made

Exeter 'the London of Devon', centre of administration and justice, with the cathedral commanding religion, and the city chamber the epitome of the county economy. Poor communications apart from by water left north Devon in some ways a distinct entity, expressed in different dialects and accents. Though there were some substantial towns there – notably Bideford and Barnstaple – more than the south the north was given over to agriculture, mostly pastoral – cattle, sheep for shearing to supply the south's vigorous cloth manufacture and trade. Across the county there were some very big landowners, but like the Russells they were mostly non-resident. Farms tended to be tenanted, small and mixed to the extent of growing vegetables.

Enclosure was well under way, increasing characteristic high hedges and deep narrow lanes concealing much of an appealing landscape. This period was one of wet summers and harsh winters – 'a little ice-age'. The Exe was frozen over at Exeter for ten days in 1670. In 1671 an ice storm coated trees which across the county collapsed under the weight. Inconsistent harvests made for market shortages, rarely surpluses. Surviving records show close connexions between annual weather and prices. Mortality could be high among sheep and cattle. Then as now farmers complained. Competition from fat Irish cattle was particularly resented. (There may have been religious undertones here.) Devon MPs were under pressure in the passage of the Irish Cattle Bill of 1677, supported by Sir Edward Seymour, the Devonian most prominent in local – and national – politics. It was opposed by Sir Henry Forde. There was a continuous economic migration into the towns, but the drift away from cob-built long houses to brick suggests that there were some prosperous farmers, employing a goodly number of labourers, if only seasonally.

Quarrying for building stone and limestone was active, as was mining for lead and copper, but tin-mining and the ancient stannaries which regulated it were already well into decline. Cloth was now the staple industry, centred on Exeter and Tiverton, but in other towns, too, where all necessary processes – weaving, fulling, tucking, dyeing – were pursued in a chiefly domestic system. Badly-housed –

cottages surviving today are those of
yeomen – and poorly-paid, cloth-workers,
both urban and rural, were also subject to
seasonal unemployment, for industry, like
agriculture, met with ups and downs.
There was a sharp cloth depression in
1680 at the height of the furore over
popery and Exclusion, which diverted
political attention from mere economics.
But generally cloth stood for prosperity
until the end of the century. Asylum
seekers – mostly Protestant from France –
brought with them their skills and
sometimes capital. The influx of Spanish
(long-staple merino) wool fostered the
production of fine serges sold in national
and international markets.

Over three decades trade was
generally buoyant in exports and imports,

both in the northern and southern ports.
Besides cloth, exports included pottery,
with its own distinctive, crudely vivid styles
from Bideford, whose more mundane
earthenware pots were used to carry
butter to South Wales, Ireland and the
New World, often topping up other
cargoes. Imports brought wine in from
France, tobacco from the English colonies
in North America, whale oil, sugar, and of
course, Spanish wool, all manner of
goods, indeed, for industrial and
domestic consumption pointing up the
purchasing power of men increasingly of
substance. Household accounts often
indicate high living. Sir Edward Seymour
stands out for his African investments
among Devon gentry with commercial
interests, which in part explains their

predilection for town houses, in Exeter
and elsewhere. Defoe, who had an eye for
that sort of thing, remarked that there
were more gentlemen even than
merchants in Dartmouth. A regular coach
service, rather expensive, demonstrated
the pull of the capital to men—and to
their women – who were well aware that
there was another world out there.

In the sixteenth century Devon
seamen had preyed on Spanish shipping.
Now they were themselves victims of the
attentions in the shipping lanes of French
privateers and Barbary pirates, as active in
their trade as they had ever been. Fishing,
local and deep water, was a vital activity,
especially for the smaller ports.
Newfoundland cod fisheries were still 'a
nursery for mariners', merchant and

naval. The royal navy would find many of its officers among the younger sons of Devon gentry. Disputes were not unknown offshore with settlers many of whom had originated in Devon.

If trade attracted pirates, it also fostered smuggling. Rife both north and south in numerous small coves and bays, with goods transported to grateful customers by horse and by night, it was confronted with only limited success by a crown anxious to maintain and extend a money supply independent of parliament. Charles II took back the Customs from the farmers, instituting a public service with a regular trained personnel. The elegant Custom House on Exeter quay employed well over a hundred officers, kept busy by increased landings resulting from the extension of

the canal to Topsham. Erected over 1679-80
by local builders in local brick to the design
of a local architect, the house displayed
high quality plasterwork ceilings devised
and moulded by north Devonians, who in
effect formed a school of some originality
and sophistication. Examples of their work
survive, notably in what remains of Monck's
house at Great Potheridge, extended by the
spendthrift second duke of Albemarle,
Christopher, last of the line. (His prime
achievement was to have been the youngest
MP ever, knight of the shire for Devon, at
the age of thirteen. He took part in debates
and sat on committees, but his precocity
did not point to a successful future. As
governor of Jamaica, got out of the way by
James II, he died of drink, aged 35).
Another surviving major Restoration

building is the Royal Citadel, brooding over
Plymouth, built in the 1670s by Charles II's
French chief engineer of works, Sir
Bernard de Gomme. Pepys thought
Gomme's elaborate structure 'rather sillily'
laid out. Certainly there were military
deficiencies in the disposition of the guns'
mountings. The Citadel would, in fact,
never be attacked – just as well perhaps.

If some deleterious aspects of the
aftermath of civil war were slow to dissipate,
lagging economic activity was not one. This
period brought wealth to enterprising men,
who, though in religion they might be of a
puritan inclination, 'worms in the eyes of
God', were not averse to some ostentatious
expenditure, notably in domestic building.
That they were open to new architectural
influences can be seen in Exeter, in

Topsham – the so-called Dutch houses – in Barnstaple and Bideford, in substantial homes, generally set at a discreet distance from the quays, themselves being extended, and away from the narrow streets, where the money was being made. Novelty was not confined to domestic housing. Town chambers put energy and public money into municipal building – workhouses, bridewells, hospitals, schools. During the 1650s some institutions in Exeter were lodged in alienated cathedral properties, purchased privately but coming officially into the hands of the chamber. After reversion to the dean and chapter some of these disappeared, but others found a necessary continuance. Across the county schools were being founded or enlarged – free schools for girls at Clyst St. George and

Barnstaple, drawing funds from charitable
foundations. The disposition of the 1635
will of the wealthy lawyer Elizaeus Hele, of
Fardel near Plymouth, was particularly
complicated. Still unsettled in the mid-
1650s, it was the subject of 'a great debate'
in parliament. In the mid-1660s it was
brilliantly manipulated by a chief trustee,
John Maynard (again), who gave a broad
interpretation to Hele's stipulation about
'pious uses'. The upshot of Maynard's legal
flexibility was to inaugurate a number of
foundations which over centuries have
evolved into Exeter and the Maynard
Schools. But he settled some funds, too, on
the borough of Bere Alston, where his
influence was supreme. All this has
prompted one historian to comment, wryly,
that a charity for the poor became

somehow a form of property in the hands of trustees to deploy against the poor.

Town defences, which had gone through many vicissitudes from long before the civil war, were over the coming years decently repaired or, more optimistically, levelled to make way for pleasure gardens, such as the aptly named Merchants' Walk in Barnstaple or at Northernhay, Exeter. Though urban slums, not an innovation of the later industrial revolution, remained a blot, chambers across the county showed their civic pride and spirit in initiating public works – drainage, sewerage, repair of bridges and highways, (always a source of disputation) flood relief, clearing of dunghills and a miscellany of other noisome nuisances tackled by official scavengers. Details are

entered into accounts, sometimes with a
comment. There seems little doubt that
urban conditions did get better, as noted
by travellers such as Cosimo, duke of
Tuscany. The cleanliness of Barnstaple air
was remarked upon and approved.
Current theory associated all manner of
diseases with bad air – and the observation
was perhaps not entirely wrong. Almost
endemic throughout three-quarters of the
seventeenth century, serious plague visited
Devon from time to time at Totnes and
Barnstaple (previously mentioned) in the
1640s and 1650. Exeter sent alms to relieve
victims of the 1665 Great Plague in
London and prudently built its own
pesthouse. Fire, too, was a constant hazard.
There were serious conflagrations in the
1660s and '70s in Tiverton, Bradninch

(forty-five houses destroyed in three hours), and at Exeter High Street and Westgate. Yet such disasters could have a helpful side, clearing areas for 'improvement' – the keyword of the developer throughout the ages – and often clearing a site for a new wing in a country house falling behind the times.

Before and after the Restoration social control was in the hands of local bigwigs – wigs were coming in at this time – reinforced by the quarter-sessions and assizes. (Even the aberrant system of Cromwell's major generals had had to call upon their co-operation and compliance.) Poverty was as ever a major – if not the major – problem not only for the poor themselves, but critically for those who had to pay poor rates. Relief was clearly necessary, but hardly to the point of offering much of comfort to the recipients. The Act of Settlement (1662) set out to stop the free passage and residence of paupers by confining or returning them to their own native parishes. It expressed an old and long-enduring social philosophy, associating poverty with crime. Magistrates tough on crime were, perhaps, not so tough in their investigations of the causes of crime. The poor were either deserving or undeserving – wilfully feckless, if not worse. Among the deserving were 'maimed' royalist soldiers – not parliamentarian – for whom there was a state-inaugurated system of relief. Devon records show a compassion and respect for such veterans. Forlorn widows might be helped with bed linen, orphans apprenticed to a useful trade. Of the undeserving, there were many categories for whom punishment from whipping to transportation was readily available. Fornication and bastardy, 'beastly lusts', were stamped upon, - with women, of course, usually taken to be the principals rather than the victims.

A survey of Devon women in the seventeenth century bears the title 'wives, widows, witches and bitches'. There was no dearth of any of these. The bitches can be found often enough slandering their neighbours, causing marital strife. The cuckold's stool was routinely repaired at Barnstaple in 1677. At the Bideford assizes as late as 1682, when the witch denunciation craze was dying out among thoughtful observers, three poor old

women, 'weary of life', assailed by yapping
witnesses, confessed to congress with the
devil, were found guilty and seen off to
enthusiastic crowds. Alehouses were often
run by women, who were sometimes
brewers, too. It was not uncommon for a
widow to take over, successfully, the late
husband's business. Some started their
own, as money lenders. Though Devon
was, like the rest of the country, under 'a
husband's law', there was more done by
women than the letter of the law and the
books of good conduct might allow.

Among 'the better sort' were women
who managed complex households,
maintained accounts, looked after estates
for absent husbands in peace and war, read
books, kept in touch with events in court,
capital and country. Newsletters, printed

and manuscript, circulated freely in Devon.
Part of the appeal of a husband in politics
– an MP, say – was the opportunity for time
in London during what would before long
settle down as 'the London season'.

Embarrassingly 'scandalous behaviour'
was not confined to the meaner sort of
people. 'Young blades' were reported as in
drink harassing respectable passers-by.
Episcopal visitation of Exeter cathedral in
the 1680s reported blatant unseemly acts
during services, shouting, quarrels, noisy
games, even children peeing in the pews
and dark corners. Sport then as now had its
hooligans. Football was (rightly) perceived
as a dangerous game. Presumably the bull-
and bear-baitings reported at Barnstaple
were more orderly occasions. Control of
alehouses was still as it had been under the

Tudors an intractable problem. In
Bideford there was one for every sixty
inhabitants. In the 1650s loose tongues
there had excoriated my Lord Protector; in
the 1670s the target might be the papist
duke of York, with healths drunk to the
duke of Monmouth. Not only tipplers
frequented these places. The Quakers, as
yet in their revolutionary phase, held their
general county meeting in 1657, referred
to earlier, at the Seven Stars Inn in Exeter.
Muggletonians, if there were any in Devon,
would sing out their hymns to jogging
popular tunes. Abstinence of the Victorian
bible-black kind was not characteristic of
seventeenth-century dissent.

At all levels Restoration society could be
rough and raffish. Yet there was another
side to it. Hating Dartmoor and its squat

people, Robert Herrick found Devon life
appealing enough to come back to Dean
Prior after his break during the
Interregnum and to feel he could still write
there loving lyrics to Dianeme and his
imaginary cohort of ladies. Defoe and
Fiennes on their rounds saw good company
and good conduct everywhere. Where
there are books, there is education,
curiosity, taste. There were booksellers in
Exeter and Tiverton, at least. Someone
must have been buying their stock. The
Cathedral library had been spirited safely
away during the troubles. It came back
intact with the revival of episcopacy and was
evidently used, not solely by the chapter.
During this period it would be augmented.
Substantial gentlemen like the Seymours,
Courtenays and Copplestone in their town

and country houses set examples of good taste and patronage to wealthy parvenus. John Dryden was a guest of Ugbrooke. A century before, Elizabeth had remarked on the courtly qualities of the Devonians she encountered. She would have found something of them still in the Restoration.

Under Cromwell and the re-installed Stuarts Devon was going through an age of transition, one of both change and continuity (which is a sort of linear change). It was a time perhaps even more than under Elizabeth I, when the county and its people were energetic, curious and interested in the national developments with which their own history was intertwined.

DEVON
FROM
RESTORATION
TO
REVOLUTION

In history there are no restorations – not complete ones, any way. In Devon, as elsewhere, between 1660 and 1688 life was profoundly affected by the ravelling up together of the immediate past, the present and of aspirations for the future. The older men who had gone to the war (or had, as some did, contrived to keep out of it) were jostled by young ones who, growing up in the destructive-formative 1650s, came of

age under Charles II. The different
experiences of different generations could
not be wished away, nationally or locally.
The ancient royal regalia had been broken
up and sold off in 1649 and a facsimile set
was rapidly got together for the coronation
in 1661. It was a symbolic gesture, emulated
in the return at Barnstaple and other
Devon towns to maces with royal insignia,
deployed in ceremonials much the same as
republican and Protectorate ones in the
1650s, themselves hardly different from
those of the Tudor century.

Monck and Grenville and their
associated Devonian old and new royalists,
instruments of the King's return, were
weighed down with honours, offices,
perquisites. Monck was returned
unopposed for the shire to the Convention

parliament, but was elevated to the Lords in July 1660. As Albemarle he was the obvious Lord Lieutenant for Devon – a vital local office in military and judicial affairs – and if he had been so inclined he could have played a major role in national politics, too. But he had the good sense to stand to one side, serving as general-at-sea in the Dutch wars and, respected by all, helping the city authorities during the Great Fire of London. Grenville as earl of Bath, governor of Plymouth Citadel, would be more directly involved in Devon and national affairs, surviving into the 1690s. The loyalty of royalists in Devon generally was more variously recognised. After the onerous 1650s – the decimation tax and all that – the old gentry came into their own again, to dominate commissions of the peace, parliamentary seats and much of local politics. Sir Edward Seymour of Berry Pomeroy, who replaced Monck as knight of the shire in the Convention and sat for Totnes in the so-called Cavalier parliament of 1661-78, assumed, after the set-back of the Interregnum, in capital, court and county the influential roles which members of his well-connected family had played over nearly two centuries. The Rolles, Drakes and Countenays were prominent once more. Old families who did not survive beyond the end of the century did so not because of the wars but because of failure to produce male heirs.

'New' men intruded during the Commonwealth and Protectorate mostly drew quietly back, but members of established families like the Northcotes

and Copplestones, who had sometimes co-
operated with the late regimes, but
overnight had become neo-royalists in
1659-60, managed to work their way back
into the charmed circle of the county
community – and to stay there. Sir John
Northcote, who had been a Presbyterian,
was elected as knight of the shire to the
Convention, sat for other seats later on and
finished up as the earl of Bath's 'cully'.
John Maynard, always in the right place at
the right time, reinforced his position, too,
quite unembarrassed by the ferocity of his
work in prosecuting those excepted from
the pardon and oblivion, among them past
associates. He sat for Exeter after a
tumultuous election for the Convention
and was somehow never out of the
Commons even until the second

Convention, that of 1689. His electoral influence in 'his' Bere Alston – he had bought the manor from the royalist earl of Newport in 1654 – throughout was supreme.

The land settlement achieved in the Convention in 1660-1 was reluctantly accepted by the succeeding Cavalier parliament – to have reopened it would have fatally impeded the ongoing Restoration settlement generally. It gave back automatically royal, duchy and church property, but had few favours for royalist families who had sold off land to pay composition and punitive fines. Even so, in reality many had, even before 1660, managed to get some of it back through covert purchases and nominees. Those who had done less well expressed their frustration by supporting the Clarendon Code, a body of legislation bearing down heavily upon dissenters – those who would not, could not, knuckle down to the monopoly of a high-flying Church of England. So was forged a lasting alliance of squire and parson, for whom dissent equalled rebellion, equalled republicanism and social disorder. Monarchy and the prayer book were the best, the only, policy. Unconformable men like Ferdinand Nicholls of St Mary Steps, Exeter, and across the county a cohort of incumbents intruded into livings over two decades, were thrown out. Like John Hammer of Barnstaple, such men would continue to preach to welcoming congregations, discreetly in homes and in illegal conventicles, meeting places sometimes

under roofs, or even out in the woods, as
from time to time at Axminster. Such
determination would clinch an English
non-conformist tradition, one already
strong in Devon, where under the loose
system of the Protectorate some had built
their own meeting places apart from the
parish churches, supported by 'ordinary
folk' but also by the consciences of men of
substance. There were, of course, those
who under the new dispensation of the
Code found it in themselves to conform
outwardly, ultimately making for a low
church persuasion. John Maynard, true to
form, was one, publicly in the church, but
in private maintaining a Presbyterian
chaplain. At Barnstaple in 1664 the elected
mayor could not take office because he
had neglected to take the holy sacrament

at least once during the preceding year. At
Tiverton in 1665 disputes over the choice
of magistrates were serious enough for the
corporation to cancel the court dinner
they loved. In 1682 several members had to
sue for pardon for taking office illegally
while not attending communion.

In August 1660 dean and chapter met
formally in Exeter Cathedral for the first
time since 1646. Down came the
'Babylonian' wall which since 1657 had
divided the nave at civil expense to
accommodate peaceably the adherents of
the two main religious factions –
Congregationalists and Presbyterians. The
bishop's throne, dismantled during the
Interregnum, was re-installed. A new
organ – the present one – would soon be
in operation. Ecclesiastical buildings,

usefully employed municipally during the
last decade, reverted to the chapter. The
new bishop, Seth Ward, would be tireless
throughout his 'reign' in securing the
interests of the diocese, which happily
seem to have coincided more or less with
his own. He was a man on his way up. Soon
chapter and city settled down to their old
none-too-easy but viable relations.

Nationally, religion was the keynote of
the intense politics of this period, as it had
been during 'the troubles'. Put crudely
cavalier and roundhead, puritan and
'orthodox' anglican – the term is
anachronistic but it is hard to hit upon a
better – would give way to 'court' and
'country' parties, accepting as badges of
honour derogatory nicknames, tory and
whig, which would give a basis for centuries

to come to a two-party political system under the monarchy, and inform politics in the localities. For tories, then genuinely 'the Church of England at prayer', their fundamental principle was non-resistance to a divinely restored monarchy. (Stand back, George Monck!). Whigs required rather more flexibility. Fear of popery, going back decades, underlay it all. A foreign policy of friendship with the catholic bigot, Louis XIV of France, produced a secret treaty (of Dover) for the conversion of England, negotiated by among others Thomas Clifford of Ugbrooke, who sat in the Cavalier parliament for Totnes alongside Sir Edward Seymour, whose influence was paramount in the borough. A talented administrator, Clifford was the 'C' of

Charles's inner cabinet, the Cabal. He went to the upper house in 1673, now a Catholic, exposed as such when his carriage overturned in a collision and a priest was glimpsed lurking inside. (It was estimated that at this time there were about 250 recusants in Devon, among them some of the Chichesters of Arlington, descendants of the Elizabethan admiral).

Anti-popery hotted up in the early 1670s when the Duke of York's long-suspected conversion became public. The Test Acts excluded papists from office (1673) and then, after the sensationalism of 'the Popish Plot', from parliament itself (1678). These measures attracted widespread support. The duke, heir apparent to the throne, was specifically exempt from the act. The Cavalier parliament was dissolved

in January 1679, under the impact of
complex issues of foreign and home policy
which presaged trouble, with moves to
exclude the duke from the highest office of
all – the kingship. During the next three
years there were three short hectic
exclusion parliaments with Charles
struggling to maintain control and to
preserve the sanctity of the succession.
Devon MPs, elected in sometimes stormy
circumstances, were divided between court
and country, tories and whigs. Some
constituencies returned one of each, as at
Dartmouth in February 1679. There the
court candidate defeated William Harbord,
'who seems to have done nothing for his
constituency in the eighteen years he sat for
it'. His court successor, Sir Nathaniel
Herne, may have seemed attractive more

for his likely local interest than for zeal against exclusion. We will never know - he died before the next election in August. In Exeter, there was great excitement for the February election, where the court candidates, one of whom was the mayor, were accused of being papists. Their supporters were harassed by a rabble of 'the inferior sort', 'fanatics', without the vote, 'well heated with drinks' shouting 'Down with the Church! down with the Chamber!' The mayor was kicked on the shins, in turn he attacked the sheriff. The exclusionist candidate, William Glyde, brewer, was elected and returned again in September, but not in 1681, when court candidates won in dubious circumstances. A Commons investigation was thwarted by the dissolution.

The exclusionists had to be defeated. Charles was as determined to maintain the hereditary succession as he was never to go on his travels again, abroad, anyway. He did manage to get down to Devon in 1670, to inspect the Plymouth Citadel, and again, in 1671. In the 1679-81 crisis he grasped that the simplest way to defeat the exclusionists was to keep them out of parliament. Here he saw possibilities, too, of extending royal influence, if not control, over local government generally, including the bench of JPs, and in the parliamentary boroughs. Devon's electorates were small – closely related more often than not to the composition of the ruling chamber, where it was (rightly) suspected that many members were actually dissenters. In Plymouth 140 freeholders determined results; in Tiverton the 25 members of the chamber; in Plympton Erle 40 freemen. What was required was to alter the town charters. This could be done, as it had been briefly earlier in the reign, by withdrawing them by writs of quo warranto for revision, chiefly of the composition of the chambers. By throwing out obvious and suspect advocates of exclusion, court and tory supporters could be put in to influence elections – or selections of candidates, for often there was no contested poll.

Actually Charles effectively defeated the exclusionists by his abrupt dissolution after eight days of the parliament called in March 1681 at Oxford, where his father had made his capital during the civil war. He immediately made his way back to London in tory Sir Edward Seymour's

coach. Proud of his lineage, certain of his
right to influence, arrogant, even, Seymour
was now the leading light in Devon politics,
but his interests were never confined to the
local. The issues were too big for that. His
effectiveness in parliament was helped by
Devon and Cornish MPs, who, working as a
bloc, secured his election in 1673 as
Speaker, the first non-lawyer to hold that
office. Anti-York agitation continued for a
while amid rumours of plots turned to the
king's advantage by subtle propaganda and
by the failure of the exclusionist whigs to
sustain the momentum of their campaign.
Even so, Charles himself did not slacken in
his onslaught. Ashburton forfeited its
charter in 1684, as did Dartmouth. At
Barnstaple there were exciting
developments. The writ was received in

August 1684. After protracted argument
the charter was surrendered in September,
to be returned, revised, with a heavy fine in
October. A year later (under James II) a
newer one still was provided. Exeter, where
Bishop Sparrow had long been worried by
the numbers of dissenters there and,
indeed, across his diocese, surrendered its
charter in August 1684. The arrival of the
new one, at the instance of the cathedral,
stressed the preservation of 'former
agreements made between the church and
the city'. Okehampton, ostentatiously loyal,
surrendered its charter in 1683; the new
one in 1684 was greeted by horsemen,
drummers and trumpeters. Plymouth,
reportedly given to choosing for
corporation membership men of 'a
meaner condition', gave up its charter in

March 1685, coincidentally, perhaps, after Judge Jeffreys had visited the town.

The effect of such electoral changes in personnel was not seen under Charles II, who did not summon another parliament before his death in February 1685. The duke of York succeeded quietly and in March called a parliament with a royalist-tory majority. But soon afterwards he had to face a possibly serious problem – a revolt in the west.

During the crisis some eyes had turned to the claims of James Scott, duke of Monmouth, Charles II's eldest illegitimate son (b.1649), fruit of a liaison which some believed then, and have since, had culminated in marriage. Dryden's Absolom, 'none so beautiful', ambitious, sharing his father's amiability but none of

his nous, susceptible to the flattery of
exclusionist politicians, Monmouth made
an ostentatiously protestant progress
through the west country in 1680 - Bath,
Longleat, Chard and into Devon. At
Colyton he spent a night with Sir Walter
Yonge, who sat for Honiton in the three
exclusionist parliaments, voting 'yes',
bringing on the crown's revengeful
regulation of the borough in 1684. It seems
that at Exeter at least ten thousand people
– 'the rabble' – turned out to see him. The
city chamber and resident gentry held
aloof. But his reception had made an
indelible impression on the young duke.
His father sent him into exile in Holland,
out of harm's way. At James's accession,
urged on by radical fellow-exiles he met
there, Monmouth decided to intervene in

England, putting himself forward as both legitimate and loyal to protestantism. He landed at Lyme in Dorset on 11 June 1685, with a small force, including veterans who had stood for 'the good old cause' during the Interregnum, still with interests deeper than merely serving Monmouth's personal aspirations. Though 'the great numbers' anticipated did not materialise, as Monmouth, under his sea-green flag, reminiscent of the Levellers of the 1640s, and confident enough to 'touch' for the King's Evil, moved into Devon some hundreds of men did join him. They were artisans, clothiers, craftsmen, labourers. More than 300 were enlisted from Devon alone – strongly from Colyton, Honiton, Luppitt, Axminster, though down to a few, even single individuals, from South

Molton, Sampford Peverell, Aylesbeare,
Bradninch and from as far afield as
Tavistock. From Exeter, where there had
been 'alehouse-talk' as early as April of
assisting the duke 'to do his business', half
a dozen came. On his landing 'a plot' by a
group of weavers, from St Sidwell's parish
had been exposed to the magistrates. It was
a really trivial affair - a few workingmen
shouting out 'A Monmouth', A
Monmouth!' and drinking his health at
Polsloe pond. Unsurprisingly, the 'plotters'
finished up in another alehouse where the
city authorities, momentarily alarmed,
easily rounded them up.

Monmouth came at a time of slump,
particularly in the cloth trade. That many
recruits were unemployed has prompted an
assertion that they joined him 'not for love

but for hopes of money'. Yet this was no
mercenary army, rather one of volunteers,
poor men, chiefly dissenters, 'an
inundation of phanaticks' fearful of popery
and despotism, but optimistic of relief from
King Monmouth. Fired by something more
than local patriotism, they saw the world in
the shape of a shilling. It should be
remembered, too, that early modern
Devon had seen a number of revolts
supported from below. Commanded by the
second duke of Albemarle, the Devon
militia, unenthusiastically dogged the
rebels' march, joined by their Somerset
counterparts, similarly 'daunted', as
Monmouth, no strategist, led his 'army' on
an erratic march ostensibly towards Bristol,
stopping at Taunton, a civil war 'nursery of
rebellion', to be proclaimed king. The fine

weather turned to heavy rain – the English
June – leading to a drop in morale,
especially when intelligence came in that
regular royal troops were on the way.
Monmouth turned back into north
Somerset. Taunton sent messages not to
come there again. At length on the night of
5-6 July the demoralised band came to
battle at Sedgemoor in the levels. It was an
ignominious defeat. The duke deserted his
fleeing troops, some of whom were
summarily executed by the victors. There
were cheers, it seems, at Barnstaple at the
news. In Dorset he was caught cowering in
a ditch. He begged, but got no mercy from
his uncle. (Parliament had already
attainted him for high treason). A botched
execution followed swiftly (15 July),
followed by a judicial 'campaign in the west'

conducted ruthlessly by 'that relentless man', Lord Chief Justice Jeffreys, his temper fired by 'the stone'. At Wells 500 rebels were 'seen off' in one day. At Taunton, Dorchester and Exeter he briskly doled out hangings, drawings and quarterings, 300 at Exeter, with bits and pieces of salted bodies stuck up on poles to dispirit treasonable imaginings. Otherwise Jeffreys resorted to the Cromwellian device of transportation. There were also confiscations of some of the well-to-do. The ascription 'the Bloody Assize' to all this was not contemporary – there was little public condemnation at the time. It took some years for a realisation of what a nasty business it had been. Jeffreys himself said later he had not been 'bloody enough for him who sent me'.

The contemporary effect of the Monmouth episode in Devon was considerable. Defeat knocked the heart out of the sort of people who had flocked to join him. Relief, if it were to come, would not be from the likes of Monmouth. If any of the Devon gentry had felt a momentary urge to join Monmouth – there cannot have been many – they persuaded themselves to wait upon events. Meanwhile, the utter failure of the Devon and Somerset militias to halt Monmouth's army made a strong impression upon the king. Having come down to the west country to see things for himself, he concluded that for security he must have an extended standing army, from 6,000 men up to about 30,000, and, better still, bring in papist officers upon whom he felt 'he could entirely depend'. This would call for a compliant parliament ready to pass appropriate legislation, enduring relief for his co-religionaries. He soon prorogued and then dismissed (July 1687) his first (tory) parliament, typified in Sir Edward Seymour. It had voted James the same revenues as Charles II and indeed, after Monmouth's rising, even more. But it was cold on a catholic-officered army. So James turned elsewhere. Coming forward apparently as a genuine advocate of religious toleration, he angled for support from dissenters by two successive Declarations of Indulgence, issued on the royal prerogative alone, suspending penalties for holding office while not receiving anglican communion. This tried hard the loyalty of non-resistance tories, who saw the country being taken over by men of a lower order – as dissenters were wont to be – and papists, eager (it was assumed) to back an untrammelled royal prerogative, that 'arbitrary government', with which James on his accession protested he had been wrongly charged. His programme was bound to affect many interests – notably protestant army officers with their careers at stake and JPs ousted from their traditional privilege of serving the community.

Further towards getting his sort of parliament, effectively a 'packed' one, James set off a systematic electoral campaign. Emulating his brother's quo warranto writs, he issued well over a hundred, this time not to put out dissenters and whigs, but tories, replacing them by papists and others who ought to be grateful to him for the opportunities he was offering them to go up in the world, or at any rate in their 'countries'. At Honiton the new charter appealed to small merchants by offering economic encouragement. (James was, in fact, acutely aware of the political value of prosperity). Gentlemen began to glimpse the makings of a social as well as a religious and political revolution in James's manoeuvres. But some dissenters would rather have toleration on a statutory basis. (That would come after 1688 in the Toleration Act.) Among men whom James did attract were some of the normally acceptable social status – like Thomas Bampfylde, hitherto only religiously and politically unacceptable. Groups of 'regulators' were sent around shire and borough, armed with questions to ask of potential MPs and holders of local offices, in county and town, about their views, if they were elected, on repeal of the penal laws on catholics. Many, caught between principled loyalty to the crown and their own interests, gave equivocal answers, hardly satisfying enough for James to go all out for a parliament. Moreover, simply by having the issues raised James was feeding discussion and debate about them.

The second Declaration of Indulgence was ordered to be read out in all churches. It was too much for many clergy. Seven bishops – Lamplugh of Exeter was not one – petitioned against the reading, to be charged with publishing a 'seditious libel'. They were acquitted by a London jury. Joy at the decision stopped in its tracks at Exeter a large contingent of Cornishmen

marching on London on behalf of one of
their own, Bishop Trelawny of Bristol. Even
after all this rebellion was not in the air. But
James was using up the positive loyalty,
month by month, of men trying to console
themselves that he was an old man in a
hurry, who would before long be
succeeded by his daughter, Mary, married
to the Prince of Orange, both firmly
protestant. To add to acts of royal power,
perceived as pushing the king 'with
precipitancy to his ruin', came the birth of
a Prince of Wales, so unwelcome an event
that it was convenient for many to profess
that the child, delivered in some mugger-
mugger, was a supposititious one smuggled
into his mother's bed in a warming pan.
(James himself put the birth down to his
prayers for a son at St. Winifred's Well in

North Wales, during a whistle-stop canvassing tour taking in Devon, the Marches, Wales and the Midlands.) The prospect now of a line of papist kings led to a carefully-worded letter sent to the Prince of Orange by six laymen and one bishop of more or less national standing inviting him to intervene in England, in effect to rescue James II and his kingdom from James II. William indicated a willingness to respond, on his wife's behalf and on his own. Involved in long-term conflict with Louis XIV, he hankered after English resources, supplied by a willing sovereign, or, if not, one 'persuaded' by apt pressures. So the last half of 1688 was an intense period of political-religious doings in England and Holland, observed with interest Europe-wide and down in the south west of

England, too. Soon William issued a declaration of intentions hinting that James was pursuing 'a regulated plan for the establishment of popery in England', including imposing 'the birth of the Prince of Wales upon the public'. (Ironically, William had previously congratulated his father-in-law on it).

James could not believe that William would invade, but invade he did, characteristically taking a calculated risk, backed by careful arrangements to ensure that while he was away his position in Holland would be secure. Over several months a substantial force was gathered – about 4,000 cavalry, 11,000 infantry of trained Dutch, French and British troops, and a fleet of sixty ships of war with some hundreds of supply and transport vessels, to be guided by twenty English pilots. Its equipment included a printing press, for a ready supply of propaganda, and a large sum of money. More outlandish was the presence of blacks from the Dutch north American settlements, in white fur caps; 'Finlanders in wild bear skins', and some camels, all under a banner with the motto ' Je maintendrai' ('I will maintain' – it went on – 'the protestant religion and the liberties of England'). Setting off on 19 October, the fleet was driven back in confusion by seasonal storms. It was in fact, rather late for a naval campaign. But within a few days, reassembled, the armada set off again, driven now by a favourable brisk wind, seemingly aiming for a landing in the north or on the east coast. But, turning abruptly into the Channel, it by-passed the

English fleet. Dartmouth and Plymouth were possible destinations, but on 5 November, the day after his birthday and a significant date in the English protestant memory, William arrived at Brixham, carried piggy-back ashore on the shoulders of a local fisherman. Though the Devon November weather lived up to its reputation everyone got safely ashore. Soon William was on his way towards Exeter, his troops trudging, soaking wet, through mud and drizzle, many of them ill from the sea passage. (Claims would be made later by the city for their nursing costs, probably never remitted.) The Prince stopped one night at the home of Sir William Courtenay, who offered hospitality, but did not commit himself. The Bishop of Exeter fled to London – where James II made him

Archbishop of York. (He would soon be in
William's service). Exonians, overcoming
their mayor's scruples, welcomed William
as on 13 November he rode on a white
horse up Stepcote Hill, armoured and
escorted. The Prince was lodged in the
Deanery while he assessed his situation.
The clergy boycotted a sermon in the
cathedral by Gilbert Burnet, who had come
over with the Prince. Both were acutely
aware of the need for some earnest local
support before moving on to test national
attitudes. At Barnstaple there was hesitancy
about reciting the Declaration issued at the
landing until someone was bold enough to
jump up on a table and shout it out. Then
news came that Plymouth had declared for
William. Soon the earl of Bath, who only
days before had erroneously assured the

king of his garrison's loyalty, would come in.
Before that Sir Edward Seymour, a more
significant figure, met William at Exeter.
The Prince courteously remarked that he
believed Sir Edward was of the duke of
Somerset's family. 'No, sir', came the reply,
'the duke is of mine.' Seymour started to
gather signatures of Devon gentry to 'an
association' for William, clinching the
invasion while the rest of the political
nation first slowly and then quickly made
up its mind. (In Devon bitter memories of
the Monmouth debacle kept the meaner
sort aloof). After a week it was apparent that
support for William and for a resignation by
James were growing. William now moved
out of Exeter. James was already facing
desertions among peers and gentry in many
parts. The royal fleet was turning against

him. 'In a perplexity' he spoke of calling a parliament – as soon as William had gone home. Coming down briefly to Salisbury James told his army officers there that he was ready to die as king of England. Defections, including that of John Churchill, suggested that fewer were ready to do the same for him. The pace of events quickened. William entered London. James, his nerve broken, fled his kingdom and his office twice, the second time successfully, encouraged by William. In the ensuing interregnum the House of Lords and the members of the last parliament assembled (December 1689) and advised the issue of writs for a free convention to settle the affairs of the nation. The elections, everywhere fought under restored charters, were lively. On the very

day that William landed at Brixham Exeter
had received news that one of James' last
minute concessions had restored its ancient
privileges surrendered in 1684 and
replaced in March 1688. The changes of
personnel then had left the city 'divided,
distracted and miserable', as the earl of
Bath reported that 'gentlemen were leaving
the city' in droves in disgust. Under the
restored charter polling for the convention
election was 'tumultuous and bitter',
though later adjudged after a Commons
enquiry 'peaceable'. It was a victory for Sir
Edward Seymour. It met in February 1689.
After long debates a majority voted that
James's departure – whether 'abdication' or
'desertion' was disputed – had left the
throne 'vacant'. It was offered to William
and Mary jointly. (William would not be his

'wife's gentleman usher' and she did not want him to be). The further settlement that followed has been called variously the Revolution, the Bloodless, the Respectable, but above all the Glorious Revolution, taken to be a foundation of our liberties.

In the Convention that brought it all about at least two of Devon's MPs were prominent. Sir (as he had become) John Maynard sitting this time for Plymouth, drawing on his selective memory, contributed thirty odd speeches to what he called the 'tormenting debates' over the desertion. Soon after election to the following parliament, he died, mourned for 'his wonderful charities and other good works' by Presbyterians, though he had once said that he was christened by the prayer book, married by the prayer book, and hoped to be buried by the prayer book. As for Sir Edward Seymour, he could not subscribe to the abdication theory, but pragmatically supported the change of monarch, since, he advised, a government of some sort was essential. A lifelong combination of principle and self-interest was aptly demonstrated in the major part he played in securing from the new king a swift deportation order on Edmund Ludlow. The exiled regicide, misjudging the nature of the revolution, had optimistically returned home. Behind Seymour's show of righteous indignation at the rogue's effrontery lay the fact that he had himself acquired Ludlow's lands, forfeited at the Restoration, and feared now he might have to give them back. He would have another decade of political life, a notable at Westminster and in Devon.

Like the Restoration, the Glorious Revolution was at once a new departure and a continuation of the past. New for Devon was the long series of wars with France that William inaugurated, which shifted the focus of naval strategy from the eastern to the western ends of the Channel. In 1690 the French bombarded Teignmouth. That would never do, so Plymouth would be maintained and nearby Dock developed into Devonport, its facilities ultimately overtaking the older port's. Above all, Torbay came into its own as safe shelter and convenient commissariat for the Fleet. In such ways the interplay of national and local affairs, which has been the theme of this brief history, would endure and, indeed, intensify.

FURTHER READING

The national context: Barry Coward, *The Stuart Age*, 2nd edn, 1994; Ivan Roots, *The Great Rebellion, 1642-1660*, 5th edn, 1995; Peter Gaunt, *Oliver Cromwell*, 1996; G. E. Aylmer, ed., *The Interregnum: Quest for Settlement*, 1972; Christopher Durston, *Cromwell's Major-Generals*, 2001; J. R. Jones, *Country and Court, 1658-1714*, 1987; Maurice Ashley, *General Monck*, 1977; Paul Seaward, *The Restoration, 1660-1688*, 1991; Ronald Hutton, *The Restoration, 1983 and Charles II*, 1985; J. R. Jones, *The Restored Monarchy*, 1979; K. H. D. Haley, *Politics in the Reign of Charles II*, 1985; John Miller, *Popery and Politics in England, 1660-1688*, 1973; W. A. Speck, *James II*, 2002; Michael Nullett, *James II and English Politics, 1660-1685*; David Ogg, *England in the Reign of James II and William III*, 1955; W. A. Speck,

Reluctant Revolutionaries: Englishmen and the Revolution of 1688, 1985; Evelyn Cruickhanks, *The Glorious Revolution,* 2000.

Devon aspects: S. K. Roberts, *Recovery and Restoration in an English County: Devon, 1649-1676,* 1985; Ivan Roots, ed., *The Monmouth Rising,* 1985; W. MacDonald Wigfield, *The Monmouth Rebellion: A Social History,* 1980; Michael Duffy et al, eds, *The New Maritime History of Devon, I,* 1992; W. B. Stephens, *Seventeenth Century Exeter,* 1958; Alan Brockett, *Nonconformity in Exeter, 1650-1875,* 1962; Janet Thompson, *Wives, Widows, Witches and Bitches: Women in Seventeenth-Century Devon,* 1993; D. Portman, *Exeter Houses, 1400-1700,* 1966; Robin Stanes, *A History of Devon,* 2nd edn, 2000; Crispin Gill, *A New History of Plymouth,* 1979; Roger Kain and William Ravenhill, eds, *Historical Atlas of South-West England,* 1999.

Works of reference: *The Dictionary of National Biography* (to be superseded in 2004); Basil Henning, ed., *The History of Parliament: The House of Commons, 1660-1690,* 3 vols (I, for general introduction, statistics, and constituencies; II-III for biographies of MPs in alphabetical order). *The Transactions of the Devonshire Association,* 1863-, and *Devon & Cornwall Notes & Queries,* 1903-, are valuable quarries of information.

Half-crown, 1670
(by courtesy of Exeter Museums Service)

Also available in the Concise Histories of Devon Series

Roman Devon	Malcolm Todd
The Vikings and Devon	Derek Gore
Devon and the Civil War	Mark Stoyle
Georgian Devon	Jeremy Black
Devon and the Second World War	Nick Smart

Also by **The Mint Press**

The Devon Engraved Series

Exeter Engraved: The Secular City (2000)

Exeter Engraved: The Cathedral, Churches, Chapels and Priories (2001)

Devon Country Houses and Gardens Engraved (2001)

Dartmoor Engraved (2001)

The Travellers' Tales Series

Exeter (2000)

East Devon (2000)

Cornwall (2000)